First English Spelling

Revised Edition

Y H Mew
Anne Seaton

Illustrated by
Tan Choon Wai
Wong Swee Fatt

LEARNERS
PUBLISHING

First edition © 2001 Learners Publishing Pte Ltd
Revised edition © 2004 Learners Publishing Pte Ltd

First published 2004 by **Learners Publishing Pte Ltd**
222 Tagore Lane, #03–01 TG Building, Singapore 787603

Email: learnpub@learners.com.sg
Visit our website: http://www.learners.com.sg

ISBN 981 4133 25 6

Printed by Sun Rise Printing & Supplies Pte Ltd

ASSOCIATE COMPANIES

R I C Learners International Limited
P.O. Box 332, Greenwood
WESTERN AUSTRALIA 6924

R I C Publications Limited (Asia)
5th floor, Gotanda Mikado Building
2-5-8 Hiratsuka, Shinagawa-ku Tokyo,
JAPAN 142-0051
Tel: 03-3788-9201
Fax: 03-3788-9202
Email: elt@ricpublications.com
Website: www.ricpublications.com

Learners Educational Publishing Sdn Bhd
43A, Jalan 34/154 Taman Delima
56000 Cheras, Kuala Lumpur
MALAYSIA
Tel: 603-9100-1868
Fax: 603-9102-4730
Email: enquiry@learners.com.my

What you'll find in this book

To Teachers and Parents

English spelling must be mastered for the full understanding of word formation in English, and for vocabulary development. Good spelling is one of the key elements of good writing.

First English Spelling has been specially written for young learners. It introduces the basic rules of spelling, covering letter sounds, noun endings such as *-s, -es, -er, -or*; verb endings such as *-s, -es, -ing, -d, -ed*; adjective endings such as *-ful* and *-less*; and the adverb ending *-ly*. Exceptions to the rules and additional information are highlighted in boxes. Much attention has been paid to the presentation and layout of this book in order to make it learner-friendly.

The book is accompanied by two audio CDs, which allow young learners to listen to the explanations and correct pronunciation. The CDs are a helpful learning tool to be used alongside the book, either at home or in the classroom.

It is hoped not only that the book and CDs will give young learners a clear idea of the basic rules of spelling, but also that they will get a lot of enjoyment from learning the varied vocabulary specially chosen for their level.

How to use the audio CDs

1. The tracks on each CD are listed below for easy reference. The page numbers given after each track refer to those in the book to help learners locate the texts.

2. The longer chapters in the book are recorded in two different tracks for quick playback of pages that learners want to listen to again. The tracks are indicated as Part 1 or Part 2 of the chapter.

3. Learners will first hear the explanations of the spelling rules on each page, followed by examples that illustrate the rules.

4. Then they will hear the notes for **Word File** and **Did You Know?**

5. There are sound effects at the following points in the CDs:

   - before the reading of the notes for **Word File** and **Did You Know?** to help learners follow the texts in the book;

   - at the end of the recording of each page to prompt them to turn to the next page.

1 The Alphabet and Letter Sounds

An **alphabet** is a set of **letters** that you use to make words. In the English alphabet there are **26 letters**, all with their own sounds. These 26 letters are arranged in a fixed order, called **alphabetical order**, or **ABC order**. You can write the letters in two forms: **small letters** or **capital letters**.

Small Letters

The **small letters** are also called **lower-case letters**. This is the way you write the small letters.

Capital Letters

Capital letters are also called **big letters**, or **upper-case letters**. This is the way you write the capital letters.

A B C D E

F G H I J

K L M N O

P Q R S T

U V

W X

Y Z

Did You Know

You use a capital letter for
- **the first letter in a sentence:** *The dog is barking.*
- **the word I:** *Tom and I are playing chess.*
- **names of people:** *Peter, John, Ali, Mary, Snow White.*
- **names of places:** *Paris, Botanic Gardens, Hyde Park, the Arctic.*
- **names of mountains and rivers:** *Mount Fuji, the Yellow River.*
- **the days of the week:** *Monday, Tuesday, Wednesday.*
- **the months of the year:** *January, February, March.*

Vowels

The English alphabet has two kinds of letters: **vowels** and **consonants.**

There are five vowels:

 a e i o u

Look at these words. All of them have a vowel in the middle.

cat	rat	mat
bed	net	hen
bin	pin	fin
log	dot	fox
mug	hug	cup

Did You Know

There are two very short words that are made up of a single vowel:

I   a

9

Short Vowels

Some vowels have a short quick sound.

In these words, the vowels are short. Read them out aloud.

a	hand	bat	man	van
e	bell	hen	nest	pen
i	fish	fist	hill	milk
o	box	cot	dog	pond
u	duck	mud	nut	sun

Did You Know

The vowel **-u-** has a different short sound in these words. Read them out aloud.

bull	bush
cushion	full
pudding	pull
pussy	put

In some words, the letter **y** sounds like the short vowel **i**. For example:

carry	city	easy
forty	lazy	party
silly	story	
baby	teddy	

10

You can put two vowels together to make a sound.

oo The pair of vowels **oo** can make a short sound like the **u** in **full**, **bull**, **bush** and **put**. Here are some words with the short **oo** sound in them.

cook	foot
good	hood
look	stood
wood	wool

ou The pair of vowels **ou** can also make the same short sound as this **u** and **oo**. Here are some words with the short **ou** sound in them.

could   should   would

ea The pair of vowels **ea** can make the same sound as the short vowel **e**. Here are some words with the short **ea** sound in them.

bread	breath	dead
deaf	death	head
	sweat	spread

Long Vowels

Some vowels have a long slow sound.

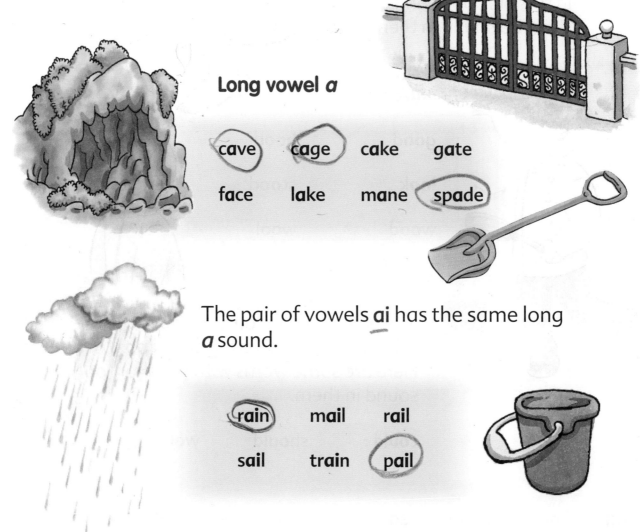

Long vowel _a_

cave   cage   cake   gate

face   lake   mane   spade

The pair of vowels **ai** has the same long _a_ sound.

rain   mail   rail

sail   train   pail

The pair of letters **ay** has the same long _a_ sound.

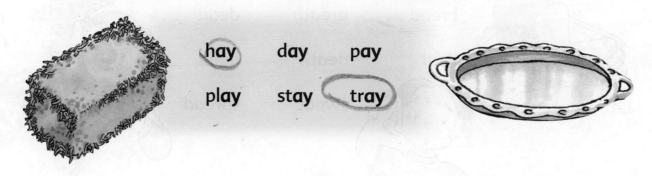

hay   day   pay

play   stay   tray

Long vowel *e*

The vowel **e** is long in these words.

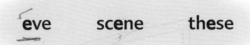

eve   scene   these

The pair of vowels **ee** has the same long **e** sound.

jeep	beef	feet
peel	see	sheep
tree	bee	

The pair of vowels **ea** has the same long **e** sound in these words.

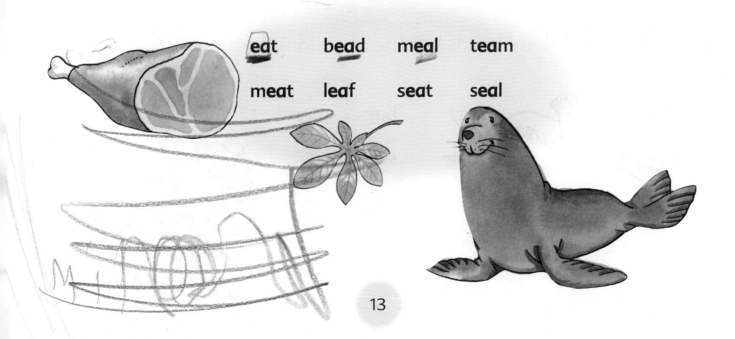

eat	bead	meal	team
meat	leaf	seat	seal

13

Long vowel *i*

The vowel **i** in these words is long.

9
nine   mice   ride

mile   kite   dive

tile   slide   wipe

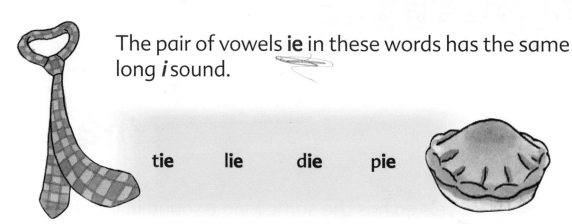

The pair of vowels **ie** in these words has the same long *i* sound.

tie   lie   die   pie

The letter **y** in these words has the same long *i* sound.

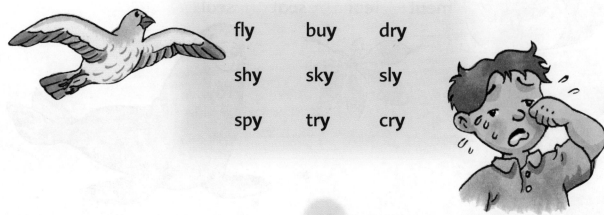

fly   buy   dry

shy   sky   sly

spy   try   cry

Long vowel o

The vowel **o** in these words is long.

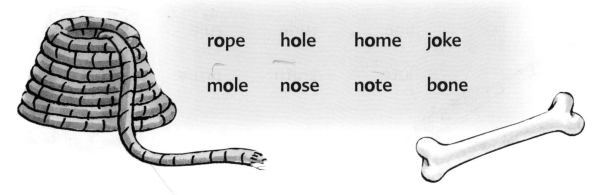

rope	hole	home	joke
mole	nose	note	bone

The pair of vowels **oa** in these words has the same long **o** sound.

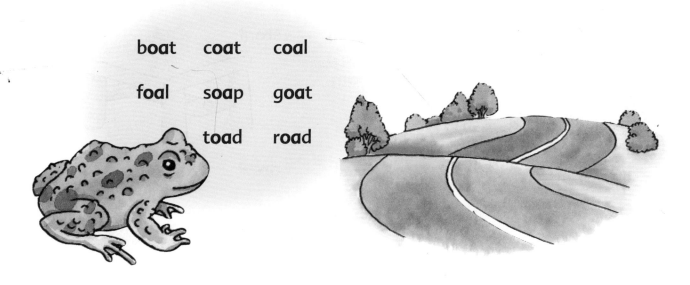

boat	coat	coal
foal	soap	goat
	toad	road

The pair of letters **ow** in these words has the same long **o** sound.

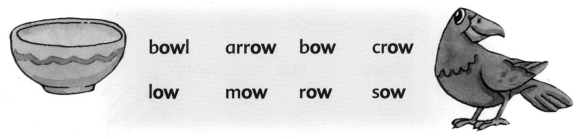

bowl	arrow	bow	crow
low	mow	row	sow

Long vowel *u*

The vowel **u** in these words is long.

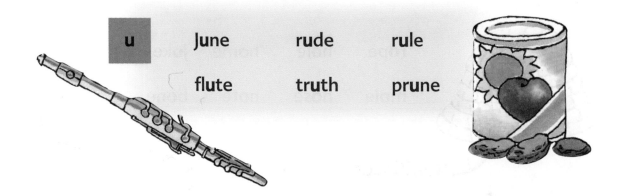

u	June	rude	rule
	flute	truth	prune

The pairs of letters **oo**, **ew**, **ue**, **ou** in these words have the same long *u* sound.

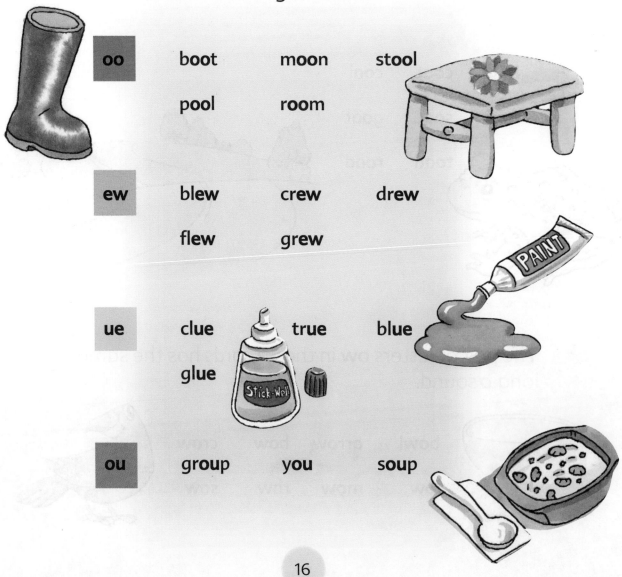

oo	boot	moon	stool
	pool	room	

ew	blew	crew	drew
	flew	grew	

ue	clue	true	blue
	glue		

ou	group	you	soup

Often **u**, **ew** and **ue** words have a **y** sound before them.

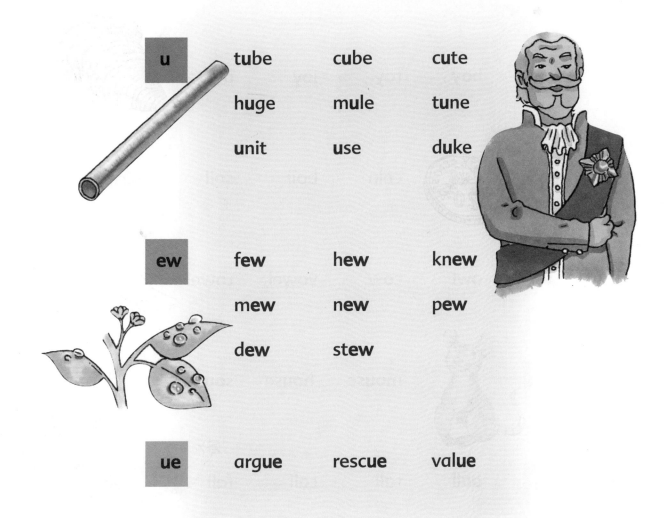

u	tube	cube	cute
	huge	mule	tune
	unit	use	duke

ew	few	hew	kn**ew**
	m**ew**	n**ew**	p**ew**
	d**ew**	st**ew**	

| **ue** | arg**ue** | resc**ue** | val**ue** |

These are some other long vowel sounds.

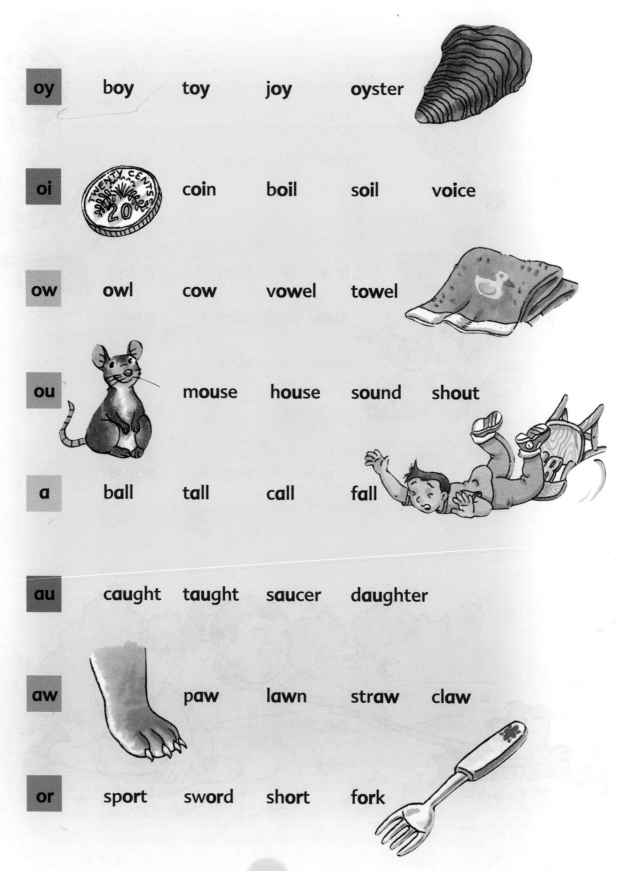

oy	boy	toy	joy	oyster
oi		coin	boil	soil	voice
ow	owl	cow	vowel	towel
ou		mouse	house	sound	shout
a	ball	tall	call	fall
au	caught	taught	saucer	daughter
aw		paw	lawn	straw	claw
or	sport	sword	short	fork

oa	roar	broad	board	oar
ou	bought	brought	sought	
a	plant	dance	chance	grass
ar	bark	farm	card	hard
al	half	calf	palm	calm
er	herd	term	serve	fern
ir	shirt	bird	girl	birthday
or	word	work	world	worm
ur	curl	burn	hurt	turn

19

Consonants

The other letters in the alphabet are called **consonants**.
They are:

b c d f g h j

k l m n p q r

s t v w x y z

Here are some words beginning with consonants.

bear	**kite**	**scarf**
car	**lamb**	**turkey**
deer	**monkey**	**van**
fox	**nurse**	**wolf**
goose	**panda**	**xylophone**
hare	**queen**	**yak**
jam	**ring**	**zebra**

Here are some pairs of consonants with special sounds.

sh

shark	sheep	shell
shirt	ship	shop
shadow	short	cushion

th

thin	thorn	thunder
thick	this	that
thumb	these	those

ph

| elephant | telephone |
| photo | graph |

Did You Know

The pair of consonants **ph** has the same sound as **f**.

The consonant **c** sounds the same as **k** when it comes before **a**, or **o**, or **u**.

calendar

cabin

camera

cobweb

cage

Word File

cab	**c**oin
cabbage	**c**old
cake	**c**ollar
calf	**c**olour
camp	**c**omb
canoe	**c**omic
cap	**c**omputer
car	**c**ook
cat	**c**ow
cave	**c**ut
cock	**c**ute

coffee

cuttlefish

The consonant **c** sounds like a **k** also when it comes before another consonant.

climb

crash

crocodile

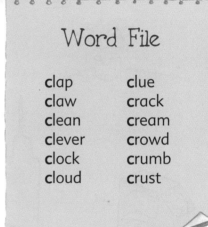

Word File

clap   **c**lue
claw   **c**rack
clean   **c**ream
clever   **c**rowd
clock   **c**rumb
cloud   **c**rust

The consonant **c** also sounds like a **k** at the end of a word.

CITY CLINIC

clini**c**

picni**c**

The consonant **c** sounds like **s** when it comes before **e**, or **i**, or **y**.

ceiling

circus

cereal

city

cyclist

Word File

celery	**c**inema
cent	**c**ircle
centre	**c**ycle
cigar	**c**ymbals

The double consonant **ch** often gives you a **k** sound.

chemist

choir

chrysanthemum

Christmas

Word File

character
chorus
me**ch**anic
stoma**ch**

The double consonant **ch** also gives you a special sound in these words.

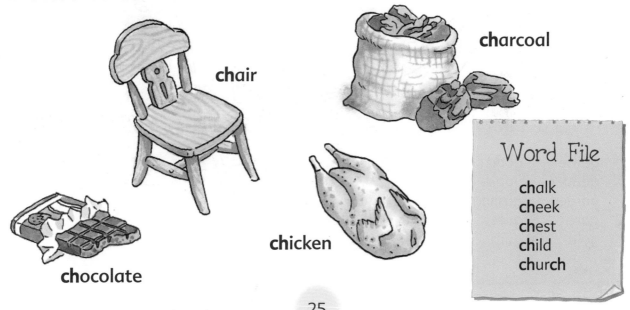

chair

charcoal

chicken

chocolate

Word File

chalk
cheek
chest
child
church

The consonant **g** has a hard **g** sound when it comes before **a**, or **o**, or **u**.

garlic

guava

goggles

gorilla

guppy

guitar

gondola

Word File

game	**g**ood
gander	**g**oose
garden	**g**osling
gate	**g**uess
gold	**g**um

The consonant **g** has also a hard sound when it comes before another consonant.

gloves

globe

graph

grapes

grandfather

grandson

Word File

glad
gloomy
glue
grammar
grass
great
green

The consonant **g** also has a hard sound when it comes at the end of a word.

bug

bag

Word File

beg   Meg
big   dig
dog   fog
mug   hug

The consonant **g** usually has a soft sound when it comes before **e**, or **i**, or **y**.

gym

gypsy

gem

ginger

giant

giraffe

Did You Know

But there are lots of words in which **g** has a hard sound before **e** and **i**. Here are some examples:

geese	**g**irl
get	**g**ive

Word File

general
genius
gentle

2 Syllables

A syllable is a part of a spoken word that you say as one sound. It usually has a vowel in it.

Some words have only **one** syllable. Here are some examples.

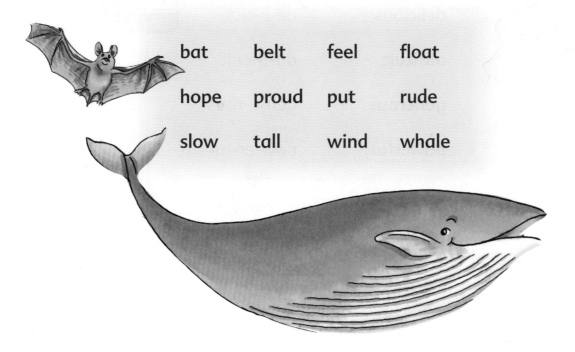

bat	belt	feel	float
hope	proud	put	rude
slow	tall	wind	whale

Some words have **two** syllables. Here are some examples.

clever	clev-er
common	com-mon
letter	let-ter
narrow	nar-row
polite	po-lite
quiet	qui-et
simple	sim-ple
stupid	stu-pid

Did You Know

If you can divide words into syllables it will help you in your spelling.

Some words have **three** syllables.

beautiful	beau-ti-ful
expensive	ex-pen-sive
delicious	de-li-cious
difficult	dif-fi-cult
generous	gen-e-rous
powerful	pow-er-ful

Some big words have **four** or **more** syllables.

comfortable	com-for-ta-ble
imaginative	i-ma-gi-na-tive
intelligent	in-tel-li-gent
interesting	in-te-res-ting
valuable	val-u-a-ble

3

Some Basic Spelling Rules

You can add the **silent e** to some one-syllable words with short vowels to make new words with long vowels.

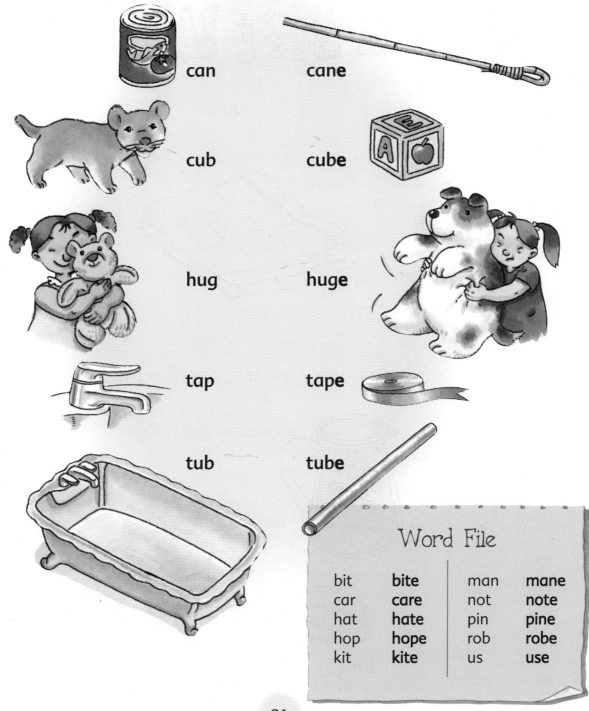

can	cane
cub	cube
hug	huge
tap	tape
tub	tube

Word File

bit	**bite**	man	**mane**
car	**care**	not	**note**
hat	**hate**	pin	**pine**
hop	**hope**	rob	**robe**
kit	**kite**	us	**use**

The letter **q** is always followed by **u.**

quill

quack

queue

quilt

quarter

Word File

quarrel
queen
question
quick
quiet
quite
quiz

The vowel **u** comes before the vowel **i** in these words.

j**ui**ce

Word File

b**ui**ld
g**ui**de
g**ui**tar
s**ui**t
s**ui**table

fr**ui**t

The consonants **c** and **k** often go together at the end of words containing a short vowel. These words have only one syllable.

clock

truck

lock

track

knock

suck

kick

Word File

ba**ck**	flo**ck**
bla**ck**	ne**ck**
che**ck**	plu**ck**
chi**ck**	sho**ck**
co**ck**	sti**ck**
du**ck**	ti**ck**

33

The consonant **k** is often followed by **e** or **i**.

kerb

kennel

ketchup

kitchen

king

kettle

kitten

kiwi

Word File

keep
keyboard
kid
kind
kindergarten
kiss

34

The consonant l is often doubled at the end of one-syllable words.

hill

wall

yell

well

drill

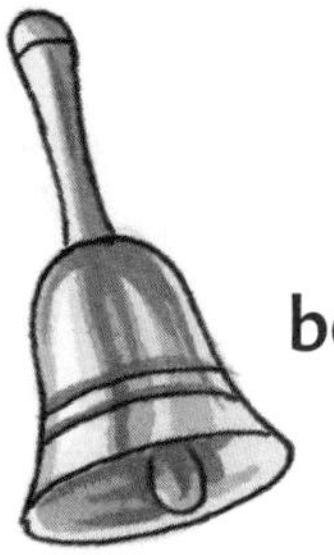

bell

pull

Word File

ball	gill
bill	hall
bull	mill
call	roll
doll	sell
dull	tall
fall	tell
full	will

The consonant **s** is often doubled at the end of one-syllable words.

che**ss**

me**ss**

ki**ss**

cro**ss**

pre**ss**

Word File

boss
hiss
less
loss
miss
pass

Did You Know

There are some exceptions:

bus	gas
is	this
was	has

The consonants **f** and **z** are often doubled at the end of one-syllable words.

buzzzz

bu**zz**

cli**ff**

pu**ff**

cu**ff**

sni**ff**

Word File

bluff   off
huff   jazz
stiff   whizz

You often find a **silent e** after **s** or **z** at the end of a word.

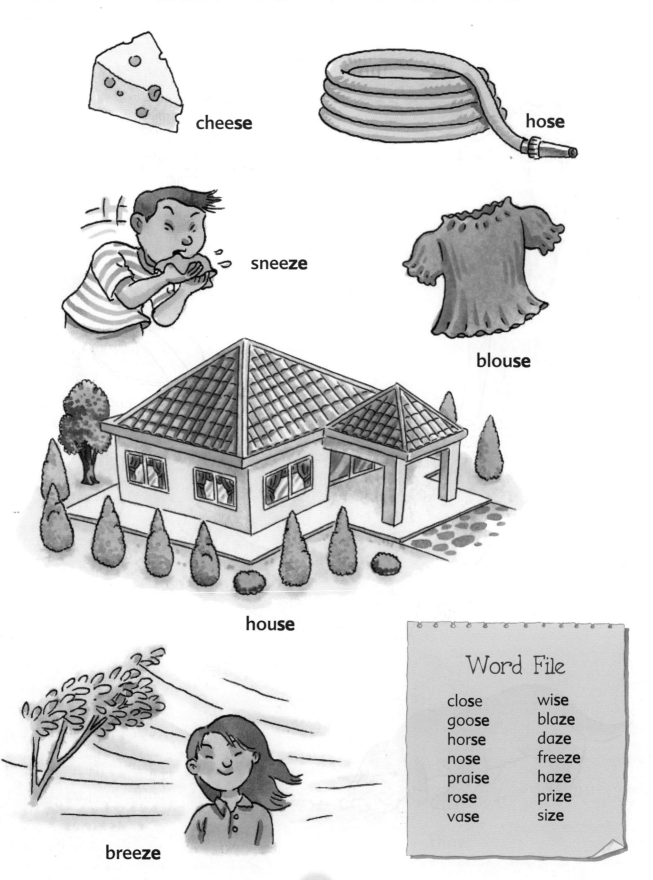

chee**se**

ho**se**

snee**ze**

blou**se**

house

bree**ze**

Word File

clo**se**	wi**se**
goo**se**	bla**ze**
hor**se**	da**ze**
no**se**	free**ze**
prai**se**	ha**ze**
ro**se**	pri**ze**
va**se**	si**ze**

In some foreign words used in English, the consonant **k** often comes before **a** or **o**.

karate

kangaroo

kampung

koala

Word File

karaoke
kayak
kookaburra
Koran
kowtow

ie or *ei*?

When the sound is **ee**, **i** comes before **e**.

field

shield

thief

Word File

bel**ie**ve

ch**ie**f

n**ie**ce

p**ie**ce

pr**ie**st

Did You Know

After the consonant **c**, **e** comes before **i**. For example:

ceiling

re**cei**ve

The double vowel **ei** can also sound like the *ie* in **pie**.
Here are some examples:

either   h**ei**ght   n**ei**ther

The **ei** can sound like the *ay* in **way**. Here are some examples:

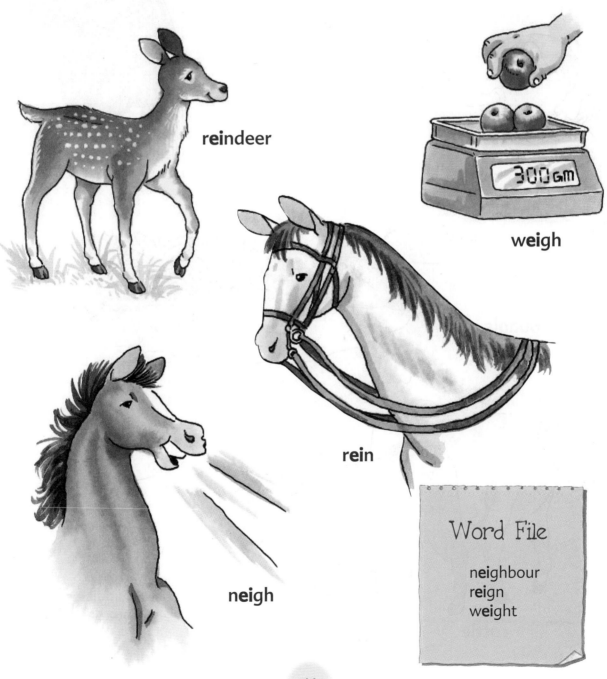

reindeer

w**ei**gh

rein

neigh

Word File

n**ei**ghbour
reign
w**ei**ght

41

Short vowel words that end in **-le** have
a double consonant before **-le**.

apple

bottle

wa**ffle**

bubble

sa**ddle**

pu**ddle**

ca**ttle**

Word File

gi**ggle**
ke**ttle**
li**ttle**
mi**ddle**
pu**zzle**

42

After a long vowel, or a double vowel, there is only one consonant before **-le**.

dou**ble**

noo**dle**

bee**tle**

cra**dle**

ta**ble**

ea**gle**

cy**cle**

Word File

fa**ble**
horri**ble**
nee**dle**
peo**ple**
sta**ble**

43

4

Spelling Rules for Nouns

From Singular to Plural

When you are talking about two or more people, animals, places or things, you have to make the singular count nouns plural.

You add **-s** to most singular count nouns to make them plural.

dragon	+	s	=	dragons
carpet	+	s	=	carpets
cup	+	s	=	cups
dancer	+	s	=	dancers
egg	+	s	=	eggs
leopard	+	s	=	leopards
school	+	s	=	schools
shop	+	s	=	shops
window	+	s	=	windows

Word File

bag	bags
bank	banks
computer	computers
dog	dogs
door	doors
drawing	drawings
floor	floors
pen	pens
umbrella	umbrellas

If the singular count nouns end in **-e**, you just add **-s** to make them plural.

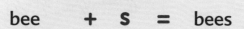

bee	**+**	**s**	**=**	bees
bike	**+**	**s**	**=**	bikes
cake	**+**	**s**	**=**	cakes
game	**+**	**s**	**=**	games
gate	**+**	**s**	**=**	gates
joke	**+**	**s**	**=**	jokes
kite	**+**	**s**	**=**	kites
plate	**+**	**s**	**=**	plates
spade	**+**	**s**	**=**	spades
whale	**+**	**s**	**=**	whales

Word File

cave	**caves**
circle	**circles**
date	**dates**
eye	**eyes**
note	**notes**
saddle	**saddles**
temple	**temples**

If the singular count nouns end in **-ge**, you just add **-s** to make them plural.

bridge   **+**   **s**   **=**   bridges

badge   **+**   **s**   **=**   badges

cage   **+**   **s**   **=**   cages

edge   **+**   **s**   **=**   edges

fridge   **+**   **s**   **=**   fridges

hedge   **+**   **s**   **=**   hedges

judge   **+**   **s**   **=**   judges

page   **+**   **s**   **=**   pages

ridge   **+**   **s**   **=**   ridges

sponge   **+**   **s**   **=**   sponges

stage   **+**   **s**   **=**   stages

Did You Know

After adding the **-s**, all these plural nouns have an extra syllable. For example:

badge   bad-ge**s**
page   pa-ge**s**
sponge   spon-ge**s**

For nouns that end in **-ch**, you add **-es** to make them plural.

beach + **es** = beaches

bench + **es** = benches

branch + **es** = branches

coach + **es** = coaches

peach + **es** = peaches

sketch + **es** = sketches

watch + **es** = watches

witch + **es** = witches

Did You Know

The word stoma**ch** does not follow this rule. You just add **-s** to make it plural.

stomach   **stomachs**

This is because the **-ch** at the end of the word sounds like **k**.

47

For nouns that end in **-sh**, you add **-es** to make them plural.

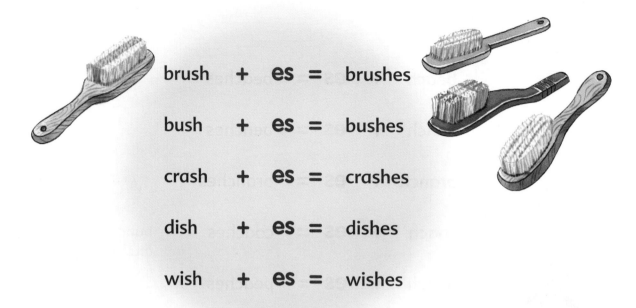

brush   **+**   **es**   **=**   brushes

bush   **+**   **es**   **=**   bushes

crash   **+**   **es**   **=**   crashes

dish   **+**   **es**   **=**   dishes

wish   **+**   **es**   **=**   wishes

For nouns that end in **-s** or **-ss**, you add **-es** to make them plural.

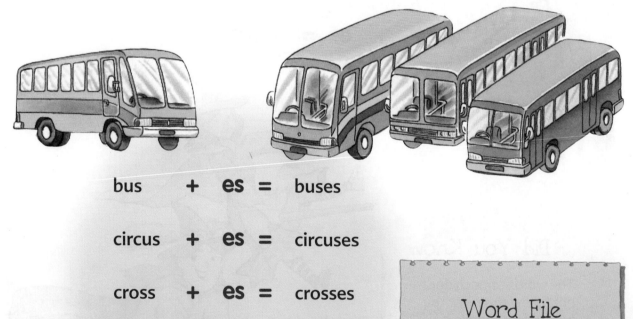

bus   **+**   **es**   **=**   buses

circus   **+**   **es**   **=**   circuses

cross   **+**   **es**   **=**   crosses

dress   **+**   **es**   **=**   dresses

glass   **+**   **es**   **=**   glasses

Word File

abacus	**abacuses**
atlas	**atlases**
class	**classes**
rhinoceros	**rhinoceroses**

For some nouns that end in **-x** and **-z**, you add **-es** to make them plural.

fox   +   **es**   =   foxes

box   +   **es**   =   boxes

fax   +   **es**   =   faxes

buzz   +   **es**   =   buzzes

Did You Know

The word **quiz** doesn't follow this rule. You double the **z** before adding **-es**:

quiz   **quizzes**

You add **-es** to some nouns that end in **-o** to make them plural.

flamingo	**+**	**es** =	flamingoes
dingo	**+**	**es** =	dingoes
hero	**+**	**es** =	heroes
potato	**+**	**es** =	potatoes
tomato	**+**	**es** =	tomatoes
volcano	**+**	**es** =	volcanoes

But for these nouns that end in **-o** or **-oo**, you just add **-s** to make them plural.

av🥑**cad**🥑 **+ s =**

av🥑**cad**🥑**s**

banjo	**+ s =**	banjos
photo	**+ s =**	photos
piano	**+ s =**	pianos
rhino	**+ s =**	rhinos
radio	**+ s =**	radios
zoo	**+ s =**	zoos

Word File

cello	**cellos**
cuckoo	**cuckoos**
kangaroo	**kangaroos**
kimono	**kimonos**
shampoo	**shampoos**

If the singular count nouns end in **-ce** or **-se,**
you just add **-s** to make them plural.

face	+	s	=	faces
horse	+	s	=	horses
lace	+	s	=	laces
rose	+	s	=	roses
slice	+	s	=	slices
vase	+	s	=	vases
dance	+	s	=	dances
palace	+	s	=	palaces
race	+	s	=	races
space	+	s	=	spaces

Did You Know

These plural nouns all have one
more syllable than their singular:

face	fa-ces
dance	dan-ces
horse	hor-ses
palace	pa-la-ces
rose	ro-ses
space	spa-ces

With some nouns that end in **-y**, you change the **y** to **i**, and add **-es** to make them plural.

cherr y i + es = cherries

baby**i**	+ **es**	=	babies
fairy**i**	+ **es**	=	fairies
family**i**	+ **es**	=	families
library**i**	+ **es**	=	libraries
story**i**	+ **es**	=	stories
strawberry**i**	+ **es**	=	strawberries

But if there is a vowel before **y**, you just add **-s** to form the plural.

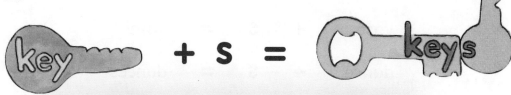

key + s = keys

day	+ **s**	=	days
donkey	+ **s**	=	donkeys
monkey	+ **s**	=	monkeys
runway	+ **s**	=	runways
tray	+ **s**	=	trays
trolley	+ **s**	=	trolleys
turkey	+ **s**	=	turkeys
valley	+ **s**	=	valleys
way	+ **s**	=	ways

With some nouns that end in **-f**, you change the **f** to **v**, and add **-es**.

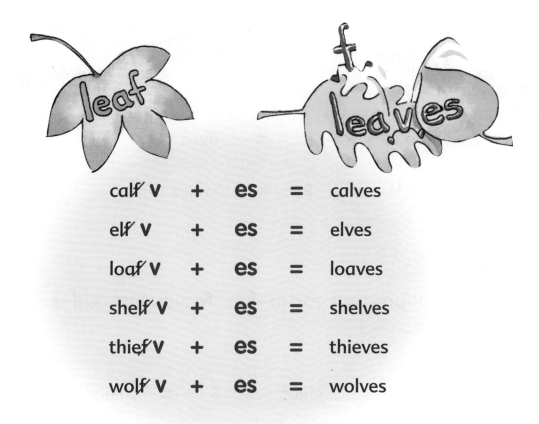

calf **v**	+	**es**	=	calves
elf **v**	+	**es**	=	elves
loaf **v**	+	**es**	=	loaves
shelf **v**	+	**es**	=	shelves
thief **v**	+	**es**	=	thieves
wolf **v**	+	**es**	=	wolves

With these words you have a choice of adding **-s** or **-es** to form the plural.

hoof	hoofs or hooves
scarf	scarfs or scarves

With some nouns that end in **-fe**, you change the **f** to **v**, and add **-s**.

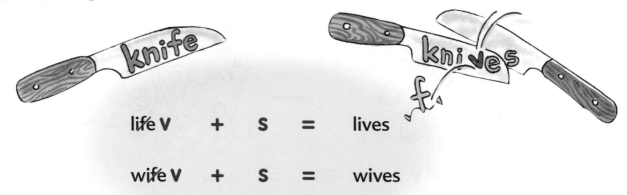

life **v** + **s** = lives

wife **v** + **s** = wives

But with some nouns that end in **-f** or **-fe**, you just add **-s** to form the plural.

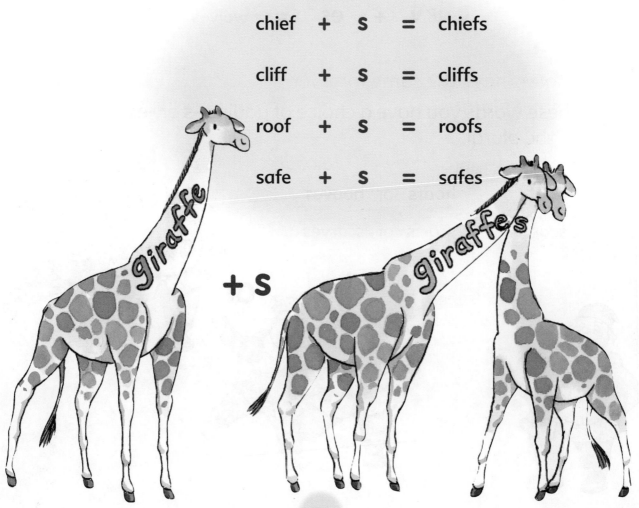

chief + **s** = chiefs

cliff + **s** = cliffs

roof + **s** = roofs

safe + **s** = safes

+ **s**

Some nouns have a plural form that doesn't end with **-s**.

mouse	—	mice
child	—	children
foot	—	feet
man	—	men
woman	—	women
tooth	—	teeth

These nouns have the same form for singular and plural.

aircraft	—	aircraft
deer	—	deer
fish	—	fish
sheep	—	sheep

Did You Know

The names of some animals have the same form for singular and plural:

carp	—	carp
cod	—	cod
salmon	—	salmon
trout	—	trout
reindeer	—	reindeer

Making Nouns

You can add **-er** or **-or** to some words to mean 'someone or something that does something'.

You can add **-er** to many verbs to form nouns.

box + **er** = boxer

call + **er** = caller

help + **er** = helper

print + **er** = printer

read + **er** = reader

sell + **er** = seller

sing + **er** = singer

ski + **er** = skier

teach + **er** = teacher

work + **er** = worker

paint + **er** = painter

photograph + **er** = photographer

But when the verbs end with a **silent e**, after one or more consonants, you just add **-r**.

bake **+ r =** baker

skate **+ r =** skater

dance	**+ r**	**=**	dancer
drive	**+ r**	**=**	driver
joke	**+ r**	**=**	joker
lose	**+ r**	**=**	loser
make	**+ r**	**=**	maker
manage	**+ r**	**=**	manager
ride	**+ r**	**=**	rider
use	**+ r**	**=**	user
write	**+ r**	**=**	writer

When verbs of one syllable end in a consonant, and have one vowel before the consonant, you double the consonant before adding **-er**.

swim + **m** + **er** = swimmer

drum + **m** + **er** = drummer

jog + **g** + **er** = jogger

rob + **b** + **er** = robber

run + **n** + **er** = runner

win + **n** + **er** = winner

With verbs of more than one syllable, you double the last consonant if the last syllable is stressed.

begin + **n** + **er** = beginner

kidnap + **p** + **er** = kidnapper

But with verbs that end in -l, you always double the l.

travel + **l** + **er** = traveller

control + **l** + **er** = controller

Did You Know

In American English, **traveller** is spelt **traveler**, with one l.

When a verb ends in **-y**, you change **y** to **i** before adding **-er** to form a noun.

cop~~y~~ **i** + **er** = copier

carr~~y~~ **i** + **er** = carrier

dr~~y~~ **i** + **er** = drier

fl~~y~~ **i** + **er** = flier

But if there is a vowel before the **y**, you keep the **y**, and add **-er**.

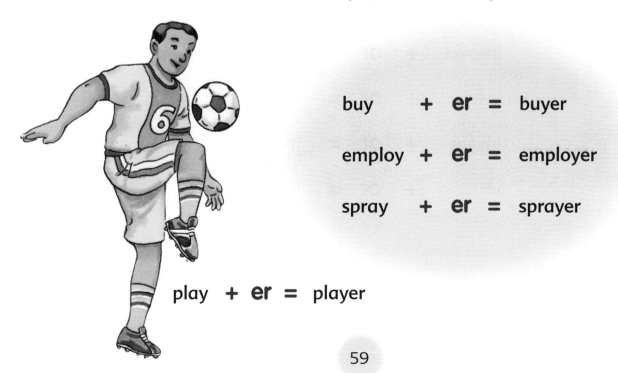

buy + **er** = buyer

employ + **er** = employer

spray + **er** = sprayer

play + **er** = player

59

With some verbs, you have to add **-or** to form nouns meaning 'somebody or something that does something'.

sail **+ or =** sailor

act **+ or =** actor

collect **+ or =** collector

conduct **+ or =** conductor

direct **+ or =** director

inspect **+ or =** inspector

instruct **+ or =** instructor

invent **+ or =** inventor

visit **+ or =** visitor

When the verbs end in **silent e**, you drop the **e** before adding **-or**.

illustrate + **or** = illustrator

create + **or** = creator

decorate + **or** = decorator

elevate + **or** = elevator

narrate + **or** = narrator

operate + **or** = operator

You can add **-ness** to adjectives to make abstract nouns. Abstract nouns with **-ness** ending mean 'the state of being something'.

sad   **+**   **ness**   **=**   sadness

dark **+** **ness** **=** darkness

fair   **+** **ness** **=** fairness

ill   **+** **ness** **=** illness

kind **+** **ness** **=** kindness

thick **+** **ness** **=** thickness

When an adjective ends in **-y**, you change the **y** to **i**, and add **-ness** to form the nouns.

happ~y~**i** **+** **ness** **=** happiness

friendl~y~**i** **+** **ness** **=** friendliness

laz~y~**i** **+** **ness** **=** laziness

lonel~y~**i** **+** **ness** **=** loneliness

tid~y~**i** **+** **ness** **=** tidiness

ugl~y~**i** **+** **ness** **=** ugliness

Did You Know

The adjectives **dry**, **shy** and **sly** don't follow this rule. For these words, you just add **-ness**:

dry	**dryness**
shy	**shyness**
sly	**slyness**

5 Spelling Rules for Adjectives

You add **-ful** to nouns to change them to adjectives. These adjectives mean 'full of' or 'showing the quality of something'.

care + **ful** = careful

colour + **ful** = colourful

harm + **ful** = harmful

help + **ful** = helpful

hope + **ful** = hopeful

use   + **ful** = useful

wonder + **ful** = wonderful

The fireworks were **wonderful**.

Did You Know

Words ending with a **silent e** keep their **e** before you add **-ful**. But there is an exception:

awe   **awful**

You drop the **e** from **awe** before adding **-ful**.

waste + **ful** = wasteful

It's **wasteful** to leave the tap running.

You add **-less** to nouns to change them into adjectives.
Adjectives ending with **-less** generally mean 'without something'.

home **+ less** = homeless
The earthquake left a lot of people **homeless.**

care **+ less** = careless

harm **+ less** = harmless

help **+ less** = helpless

hope **+ less** = hopeless

leaf **+ less** = leafless

seed **+ less** = seedless

spot **+ less** = spotless

use **+ less** = useless

With nouns that end in **-y**, you change the **y** to **i** before adding **-ful** or **-less**.

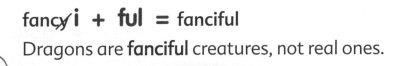

fanc~~y~~**i** + **ful** = fanciful

Dragons are **fanciful** creatures, not real ones.

beaut~~y~~**i** + **ful** = beautiful

merc~~y~~ **i** + **ful** = merciful

pit~~y~~ **i** + **ful** = pitiful

penn~~y~~i + **less** = penniless

Jim had spent all his pocket money, so he was **penniless**.

merc~~y~~**i** + **less** = merciless

pit~~y~~**i** + **less** = pitiless

But when there is a vowel before **-y**, you keep the **y**, and add **-ful** or **-less**.

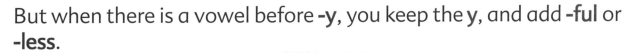

joy	+	**ful**	=	joyful
play	+	**ful**	=	playful
joy	+	**less**	=	joyless
money	+	**less**	=	moneyless

Adjectives that end with **-able** and **-ible** mean 'that you can do something to'. You can add **-able** to many verbs to form adjectives.

break **+ able** = breakable
Glass is a **breakable** material.

enjoy **+ able** = enjoyable
read **+ able** = readable
wash **+ able** = washable

These adjectives are spelt with **-ible** ending.

sensible
terrible
visible

horrible
I think there's a **horrible** monster under my bed.

Here are more adjectives that end with **-able** or **-ible**.

comfortable   responsible
reasonable   suitable

66

With some verbs ending in **-e**, you drop the **e** before adding **-able**.

cure + **able** = curable

use + **able** = usable

value + **able** = valuable

adore + **able** = adorable
What an **adorable** little baby!

With other verbs ending in **-e**, you keep the **e** and add **-able**.

notice + **able** = noticeable
There was a **noticeable** lump in the bed.

change + **able** = changeable

These adjectives can be spelt with or without **e** before **-able**.

love   loveable or lovable

move   moveable or movable

like   likeable or likable
Kent is a **likeable** (or **likable**) boy.

67

Adjectives that end with **-y** generally mean 'having a lot of something'. You can add **y** to many nouns to form adjectives.

air   **+ y =** airy

cloud   **+ y =** cloudy

dirt   **+ y =** dirty

dust   **+ y =** dusty

health **+ y =** healthy

rain   **+ y =** rainy

rust   **+ y =** rusty

storm   **+ y =** stormy

sand **+ y =** sandy

We found a nice **sandy** beach for our swim.

wind **+ y =** windy

It often gets **windy** in the afternoons here.

Word File

gloom	**gloomy**
hair	**hairy**
luck	**lucky**
mess	**messy**
milk	**milky**
mood	**moody**
oil	**oily**
snow	**snowy**

With nouns that end with a **silent e**, you drop the **e**, and add **-y**.

bubbl**e** **+** **y** **=** bubbly
Do you like **bubbly** drinks such as Coke?

breez**e** **+** **y** **=** breezy

eas**e** **+** **y** **=** easy

haz**e** **+** **y** **=** hazy

juic**e** **+** **y** **=** juicy

nois**e** **+** **y** **=** noisy

ros**e** **+** **y** **=** rosy

smok**e** **+** **y** **=** smoky

ston**e** **+** **y** **=** stony

tast**e** **+** **y** **=** tasty

wav**e** **+** **y** **=** wavy
Can you draw a **wavy** line?

With nouns that have only one vowel and end with a consonant, you double the consonant before adding **-y**.

fur **+ r + y =** furry

This coat has a **furry** collar and cuffs.

fog	**+ g**	**+ y**	**=**	foggy
fun	**+ n**	**+ y**	**=**	funny
mud	**+ d**	**+ y**	**=**	muddy
skin	**+ n**	**+ y**	**=**	skinny
star	**+ r**	**+ y**	**=**	starry
sun	**+ n**	**+ y**	**=**	sunny

bag **+ g + y =** baggy

Sam is wearing a pair of very **baggy** jeans.

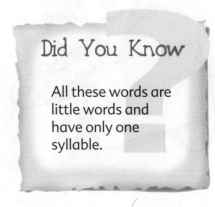

Did You Know

All these words are little words and have only one syllable.

6 Spelling Rules for Adverbs

Many adverbs are spelt with an **-ly** at the end.
You form them by adding **-ly** to adjectives.

sad + **ly** = sadly

Granny waved goodbye **sadly** as we left.

brave   + **ly** = bravely

free   + **ly** = freely

foolish + **ly** = foolishly

kind   + **ly** = kindly

neat   + **ly** = neatly

nice   + **ly** = nicely

proud   + **ly** = proudly

quick   + **ly** = quickly

quiet   + **ly** = quietly

slow   + **ly** = slowly

If the adjectives end in **-y**, you have to change the **y** to **i** before adding **-ly**.

angr~~y~~ **i** + **ly** = angrily

The policeman spoke **angrily** to the driver.

busy **i** + **ly** = busily

easy **i** + **ly** = easily

greedy **i** + **ly** = greedily

hasty **i** + **ly** = hastily

heavy **i** + **ly** = heavily

lazy **i** + **ly** = lazily

lucky **i** + **ly** = luckily

merry **i** + **ly** = merrily

tidy **i** + **ly** = tidily

We put the books **tidily** back on the shelves.

When you add **-ly** to adjectives that end in **-ful**, remember that you get **-ll-**.

tearful **+** **ly** = tearfully

'My watch is broken,' said David **tearfully**.

beautiful **+** **ly** = beautifully

careful **+** **ly** = carefully

cheerful **+** **ly** = cheerfully

faithful **+** **ly** = faithfully

graceful **+** **ly** = gracefully

hopeful **+** **ly** = hopefully

joyful **+** **ly** = joyfully

painful **+** **ly** = painfully

peaceful **+** **ly** = peacefully

pitiful **+** **ly** = pitifully

playful **+** **ly** = playfully

useful **+** **ly** = usefully

Did You Know?

If the adjectives end in -ll, you just add -y.

full   **fully**

If the adjectives end in **-le**, you just change the **e** to **y** to form adverbs.

singl~~e~~ **+ y =** singly

Come forward **singly** as I read out your name.

comfortabl~~e~~ **+ y =** comfortably

gentl~~e~~ **+ y =** gently

horribl~~e~~ **+ y =** horribly

humbl~~e~~ **+ y =** humbly

possibl~~e~~ **+ y =** possibly

sensibl~~e~~ **+ y =** sensibly

simpl~~e~~ **+ y =** simply

terribl~~e~~ **+ y =** terribly

7 Spelling Rules for Verbs

The Third Person Singular

You put **-s** at the end of most verbs when you use them with the pronouns **he**, **she** and **it**, and with **singular nouns**. The -s form of the verbs is known as the **third person singular**.

travel **+ S** = travels

Mum is a school inspector, so she **travels** a lot.

bend **+ S** = bends

This branch is not strong. It **bends** easily.

help **+ S** = helps

Chris often **helps** his mother with the housework.

bark **+ S** = barks

build **+ S** = builds

draw **+ S** = draws

drink **+ S** = drinks

hide **+ S** = hides

open **+ S** = opens

play **+ S** = plays

You add **-es** instead of **-s** to verbs that end in **-sh** and **-ss**, to form the third person singular.

pass **+ es =** passes

The bus **passes** our house every morning at eight o'clock.

brush **+ es =** brushes

Paul always **brushes** his teeth after breakfast.

crash **+ es =** crashes

finish **+ es =** finishes

push **+ es =** pushes

vanish **+ es =** vanishes

wash **+ es =** washes

cross + es = crosses

Sue always looks both ways before she **crosses** over.

dress + **es** = dresses

hiss + **es** = hisses

miss + **es** = misses

polish + es = polishes

Dad **polishes** his shoes till they shine.

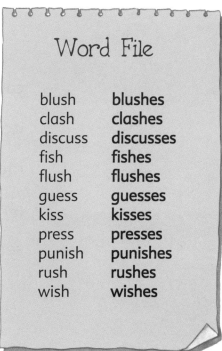

Word File

blush	**blushes**
clash	**clashes**
discuss	**discusses**
fish	**fishes**
flush	**flushes**
guess	**guesses**
kiss	**kisses**
press	**presses**
punish	**punishes**
rush	**rushes**
wish	**wishes**

You add **-es** instead of **-s** to verbs that end in **-ch** to form the third person singular.

fetch **+ es =** fetches

Dad **fetches** us from our swimming class on a Thursday.

catch **+ es =** catches

itch **+ es =** itches

march **+ es =** marches

pinch **+ es =** pinches

search **+ es =** searches

watch + es = watches

Our cat **watches** the birds from the window, longing to chase them.

hatch + es = hatches

The chick breaks through the shell as it **hatches** out.

attach + **es** = attaches

match + **es** = matches

punch + **es** = punches

reach + **es** = reaches

snatch + **es** = snatches

stitch + **es** = stitches

stretch + **es** = stretches

teach + **es** = teaches

touch + **es** = touches

You add **-es** to verbs that end in **-o**, **-x** and **-z** to form the third person singular.

do **+ es =** does

Sue **does** her exercises in front of the mirror every morning.

buzz **+ es =** buzzes

A bee is a large insect. It **buzzes** only when it flies.

echo **+ es =** echoes

fax **+ es =** faxes

fizz **+ es =** fizzes

go **+ es =** goes

mix **+ es =** mixes

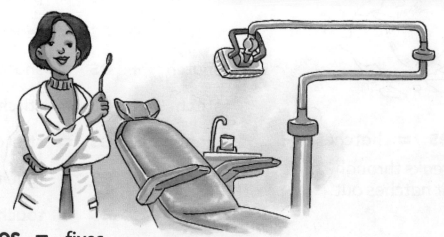

fix **+ es =** fixes

The dentist **fixes** your teeth when you get holes in them.

With verbs that end in **-y** and have a consonant before the **y**, you change **y** to **i**, and add **-es** to form the third person singular.

bur~~y~~ **i** + **es** = buries

Our dog **buries** the bones in the garden.

marr~~y~~ **i** + **es** = marries

A girl is called a bride when she **marries.**

carr~~y~~ **i** + **es** = carries

I like my big brother. He often **carries** me on his shoulders.

cop~~y~~ **i** + **es** = copies

cr~~y~~ **i** + **es** = cries

dr~~y~~ **i** + **es** = dries

stud~~y~~ **i** + **es** = studies

tr~~y~~ **i** + **es** = tries

worr~~y~~ **i** + **es** = worries

fl~~y~~ **i** + **es** = flies

This plane **flies** to and from Britain every day.

But you don't drop the **y** if there is a vowel **a**, **e**, **o** or **u** before it. You just add **-s** after the **y**.

pay + S = pays

Each customer **pays** for their goods at the checkout.

say + S = says

This notice **says** 'Keep left'.

annoy **+ S =** annoys

buy   **+ S =** buys

lay   **+ S =** lays

obey **+ S =** obeys

play **+ S =** plays

stay **+ S =** stays

enjoy + S = enjoys

A puppy **enjoys** being patted and played with.

The Present Participle

The **-ing** form of verbs is called the **present participle** or **gerund**. You use it to make the continuous tense.

With most verbs, you just add **-ing**.

fish **+ ing =** fishing

read **+ ing =** reading

drink **+ ing =** drinking

eat **+ ing =** eating

fly **+ ing =** flying

play **+ ing =** playing

shoot **+ ing =** shooting

sing **+ ing =** singing

sleep **+ ing =** sleeping

With verbs that end with an **-e**, you usually have to drop the **e** before you add **-ing**.

shake + **ing** = shaking
We were all **shaking** with laughter.

chase + **ing** = chasing
The dog was **chasing** the cat around the garden.

drive + **ing** = driving
Dad is **driving** the car through the gates.

cycle + **ing** = cycling
Fred is **cycling** along the path.

ride + **ing** = riding

rise + **ing** = rising

share + **ing** = sharing

take + **ing** = taking

wave + **ing** = waving

With verbs that have only one short vowel, and end with a consonant, you have to double the last consonant before adding **-ing**.

fan **+ n + ing =** fanning

Helen is **fanning** herself because she is too hot.

jog **+ g + ing =** jogging

People are **jogging** around the park.

clap **+ p + ing =** clapping

hop **+ p + ing =** hopping

hug **+ g + ing =** hugging

rub **+ b + ing =** rubbing

stop **+ p + ing =** stopping

pat **+ t + ing =** patting

I'm **patting** my dog's head.

Word File

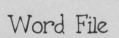

beg	**begging**
chat	**chatting**
drop	**dropping**
hum	**humming**
nod	**nodding**
plan	**planning**
rob	**robbing**
swim	**swimming**
tap	**tapping**
wag	**wagging**

Did You Know

These verbs have only one syllable. They end with consonants such as **b, d, g, m, n, p** or **t**.

With verbs of more than one syllable that end with the consonant **l**, and with one vowel before the **l**, you always double the **l** before adding **-ing**.

control **+ l + ing** = controlling

A policeman is **controlling** the traffic at the crossing.

travel **+ l + ing** = travelling

We were **travelling** in Europe when our coach broke down.

cancel **+ l + ing** = cancelling

patrol **+ l + ing** = patrolling

pedal **+ l + ing** = pedalling

signal **+ l + ing** = signalling

Did You Know

In American English you do not double the **l** before adding **-ing**:

cancel	**canceling**
label	**labeling**
pedal	**pedaling**
signal	**signaling**
travel	**traveling**

You just add **-ing** to verbs that end in **-ee**, **-oe** or **-ye**.

agree **+ ing =** agreeing

free **+ ing =** freeing

see **+ ing =** seeing

flee **+ ing =** fleeing

We were all **fleeing** from the angry wasps.

dye **+ ing =** dyeing

eye **+ ing =** eyeing

tiptoe **+ ing =** tiptoeing

canoe **+ ing =** canoeing

We spent a week **canoeing** along the river.

With verbs ending in **-ie**, you change **ie** to **y** before adding **-ing**.

li~~e~~ **y + ing =** lying

ti~~e~~ **y + ing =** tying

di~~e~~ **y + ing =** dying

I think these flowers are **dying**.

The Past Participle

You usually add **-ed** to the verbs to make the simple past tense and past participle.

boil + **ed** = boiled
We **boiled** the dumplings in a big pot.

jump + **ed** = jumped
We **jumped** into the swimming pool one by one.

bark   + **ed** = barked

clean + **ed** = cleaned

comb + **ed** = combed

cook   + **ed** = cooked

help   + **ed** = helped

pick   + **ed** = picked

talk   + **ed** = talked

cross + **ed** = crossed
Dave **crossed** the road using the pedestrain crossing.

You just add **-d** to most verbs that end with an **-e** to form the simple past tense.

queue + d = queued

We **queued** for two hours for tickets for the match.

blame	+ d	=	blamed
change	+ d	=	changed
chase	+ d	=	chased
close	+ d	=	closed
cycle	+ d	=	cycled
dance	+ d	=	danced
gaze	+ d	=	gazed
hope	+ d	=	hoped
like	+ d	=	liked
paddle	+ d	=	paddled

Here are more verbs that end in **-e**. With these verbs you just add **-d** to form the simple past tense.

paste + **d** = **pasted**
I've **pasted** all these pictures into my scrapbook.

bake + **d** = **baked**
Mike has **baked** a butter cake.

dive   + **d** = dived

divide   + **d** = divided

glance   + **d** = glanced

guide   + **d** = guided

invite   + **d** = invited

live   + **d** = lived

love   + **d** = loved

note   + **d** = noted

notice   + **d** = noticed

receive + **d** = received

recite   + **d** = recited

Did You Know

If the verb ends with the sound **d** or **t**, the simple past tense has an extra syllable. Here are some examples:

divided	di-vi-ded
guided	gui-ded
invited	in-vi-ted
noted	no-ted
recited	re-ci-ted

With verbs that have one vowel and end with a consonant, you have to double the last consonant before adding **-ed** to form the simple past tense.

pin **+ n + ed =** pinned

Sally **pinned** the flower to her dress.

grab **+ b + ed =** grabbed

I **grabbed** an orange to take with me for lunch.

slam **+ m + ed =** slammed

Tom **slammed** the door angrily.

dot	**+ t**	**+ ed**	**=**	dotted
drop	**+ p**	**+ ed**	**=**	dropped
fan	**+ n**	**+ ed**	**=**	fanned
fit	**+ t**	**+ ed**	**=**	fitted
nag	**+ g**	**+ ed**	**=**	nagged
nod	**+ d**	**+ ed**	**=**	nodded
spot	**+ t**	**+ ed**	**=**	spotted
stop	**+ p**	**+ ed**	**=**	stopped

Did You Know

These verbs have only one syllable. If the verbs end with the sound *d* or *t*, you get the extra syllable in the simple past tense. Here are some examples:

fitted	fit-ted
nodded	nod-ded
spotted	spot-ted

With verbs that end in **-y**, you change the **y** to **i**, and add **-ed** to form the simple past tense.

carry **i + ed =** carried

Helen **carried** the tray of drinks out into the garden.

hurry **i + ed =** hurried

I **hurried** along the pavement to catch the bus.

bury**i** + **ed** = buried

We **buried** Dad up to his neck in the sand.

cry**i** + **ed** = cried

dirty**i** + **ed** = dirtied

dry**i** + **ed** = dried

empty**i** + **ed** = emptied

fry**i** + **ed** = fried

pity**i** + **ed** = pitied

reply**i** + **ed** = replied

tidy**i** + **ed** = tidied

try**i** + **ed** = tried

spy**i** + **ed** = spied

We **spied** a bird sitting on the top branch of the tree.

If a verb has a vowel before the **y**, you just add **-ed** to form the simple past tense.

enjoy + **ed** = enjoyed
We all **enjoyed** the circus.

destroy + **ed** = destroyed
The storm has **destroyed** the crops.

sway + **ed** = swayed
The trees **swayed** to and fro in the wind.

annoy + **ed** = annoyed

employ + **ed** = employed

obey + **ed** = obeyed

play + **ed** = played

pray + **ed** = prayed

stay + **ed** = stayed

Did You Know
These verbs don't follow this rule.
lay   **laid**
pay   **paid**
say   **said**
They are called **irregular verbs**.

If the verbs end in the consonant **l**, and there is a single vowel before it, you always double the **l** before adding **-ed**.

patrol + l + ed = patrolled
Police cars **patrolled** the streets every night.

pedal + l + ed = pedalled
Katie **pedalled** her tricycle round the garden.

signal + l + ed = signalled
Dad **signalled** that he was turning left.

cancel + l + ed = cancelled

control + l + ed = controlled

travel + l + ed = travelled

Many verbs in English do not add **-ed** to form the simple past tense and past participle. These verbs are called **irregular verbs**.

Here are some irregular verbs.

Base Form	Simple Past	Past Participle
blow	blew	blown
break	broke	broken
build	built	built
cut	cut	cut
dig	dug	dug
draw	drew	drawn
drink	drank	drunk
drive	drove	driven
eat	ate	eaten
give	gave	given
hide	hid	hidden
hurt	hurt	hurt
lose	lost	lost
ring	rang	rung
shut	shut	shut
teach	taught	taught